THE AH! WISDOM BOOK

Conversations with
Swami Tejomayananda

Find out more about
Chinmaya Mission
by visiting the website at
www.chinmayamission.com

First Edition: June 2010. 15,000 copies

Publisher
Central Chinmaya Mission Trust
Saki Vihar Road, Mumbai - 400072, India.
Tel: 91 (22) 28572367/28575806   Fax: 91 (22) 28573065
Email: ccmtpublications@chinmayamission.com
Website: www.chinmayamission.com

Distribution Centre in USA
Chinmaya Mission West Publications Division
560 Bridgetown Pike
Langhorne, PA 19053, USA
Tel: (215) 3960390   Fax: (215) 3969710
Email: publications@chinmaya.org
Website: www.chinmayapublications.org

Cover design and layout
Zoe Collington, Preeti Pahwa

Printed by
Thomson Press
Thane Belapur Road, Airoli
Navi Mumbai 400 708, India

Price: Rs. 150/-
ISBN: 9788175974883

In these topsy turvy times,
When the world seems upside down;
Nothing makes things quite so clear,
As the wisdom of Swami Tejomayananda.

An offering of love

to

Guruji

from the devotees of Chinmaya Mission.

Contents

CONTENTS

Preface

In folk tales, a sage often appears homeless, wearing ragged clothes and funny shoes.

But this is not a folk tale. This is about a REAL sage. Most real sages look very much like ordinary people. They live in ordinary homes and work in ordinary jobs. *Only, they do things extraordinarily.*

In these short stories, an attempt has been made to capture the resplendence of a real sage – Swami Tejomayananda. As head of Chinmaya Mission, he is much sought after. Yet in his everyday interactions, Guruji is at perfect ease with his surroundings. The depth of his personality is vividly seen in his wisdom, wit and simplicity.

These 73 stories have been selected from over 600 that were gathered from devotees of Chinmaya Mission around the world, to be presented to Guruji in this surprise book, as a token of love and appreciation.

Each of these stories is true, although some editing was necessary in exercising creative licence.

The explanations at the end of each story are sourced from the works of Masters, namely, Swami Chinmayananda (Founder, Chinmaya Mission), Swami Chidananda (President, Divine Life Society) and Swami Tejomayananda (Head, Chinmaya Mission). Our humble salutations and thanks to them.

We thank the main sponsors of *The Ah! Wisdom Book:* Harish, Lakshmi & Sacheen Hiranand, Bela Pandya, Chinmaya Seva Centre Singapore, Arvind & Meena Mathur, Rajbir & Nicki Singh and Gopala & Shashikala Dwarkanath. We also thank the many others who have generously contributed and worked to put this book together. And, a special note of appreciation for the talented cartoonist, who wishes to stay anonymous.

30 June 2010   Books and Publications Division
Mumbai, 400 072   Central Chinmaya Mission Trust

Introducing

Swami Tejomayananda
as Guruji

The Wiseman
playing the part of Guruji

When does
life begin?

A very thick parcel arrived by post for Guruji. He cut it open and pulled out pages of perfectly typed jokes.

"You have to read five hundred and you get four nice ones!" said an amused Guruji. He started to read them out aloud.

> "A swami, a priest and a rabbi are asked the question: When does life begin?
>
> Swami: The moment of conception.
>
> Priest: The moment of birth.
>
> Rabbi: The moment the children are married and all the loans and mortgages have been paid off."

"Ha! Ha!" laughed some people who were sitting there.

"This one is okay*ish,* Guruji," said one person. "It's an interesting question!"

"Guruji, if I were to ask you," the person continued, "what would your answer be? *When does life begin?*"

"At the moment of Self-Realization," replied Guruji.

"Oooooh! That's a lovely answer."

"That is my answer in the *absolute* sense," continued Guruji. "In the *relative* sense, life begins the moment you have the desire for Self-Realization. Because, then it's only a matter of time."

"That's why I keep saying, don't worry so much about your day to day experiences. They are meaningless. Only when you have understood that they are meaningless, then does the meaningless become meaningful."

The desire for Self-Realization is the turning point in the spiritual life of man. The moment he starts to question the validity of the pursuits he has been following, he becomes a seeker. Once the desire comes, it is then a natural progression to the final destination. This awakening, this urge for Self-Realization, is the movement of God within us. As long as we (the ego) persist, we continue to hamper this movement. It is in the dying of the little self that we attain everlasting life. And it is only then, that each moment in life becomes all that it ought to be, an ascending step, a manifestation of a brighter light from within. Just as rainwater flows through the river and merges into the sea, from where it originated; in the same way the jīva (individual ego), that has sprung from the supreme Self, rests only when it reaches its source.

Real new
world

One day in 1985, Brahmacārī[1] Vivek Chaitanya[2] arrived at a house where he often stayed in New Delhi. The entire family was astonished to see him, for he looked a different man. His head had been recently tonsured, and his robes were no longer yellow, but a deep saffron colour. He had been blessed with the holy order of sannyāsa.[3] Seeing the surprised looks, Swami Tejomayananda gave a big smile, and even bigger hugs to all.

Resplendent in his ochre robes, he sat down for breakfast. "One time, when I was a brahmacārī," he recalled at the table, "one small child had run up to his mother shouting 'Mummy! Mummy! **Bhram** cārī ji has come'."

"The name, 'Bhrama cārī'[4] means: he who dwells in illusion," said Swamiji. "I used to wonder at the truth of what the boy had said in his innocence."

Everyone had a hearty laugh. "At least, now the boy

---

[1] spelt as brahmacārī: one pursuing the knowledge of Brahman; one who lives a student life | [2] Guruji's name as a brahmacārī | [3] path of renunciation | [4] spelt as bhrama cārī: one on the path of illusion

cannot call me **bhra***m* cārī anymore!" said Swamiji with a chuckle.

"Swamiji, what difference do you find in the life of a sannyāsi from that of a brahmacārī?" asked a family member.

With a huge smile, Swamiji looked up mischievously and answered: "Ah! That yellow yellow dirty fellow is no more!"

Sannyāsa is the renunciation of the ego and desires for the world. In the literal sense, when an individual takes sannyāsa, he performs his last rites in the world as an individual. From a spiritual standpoint, true sannyāsa implies Self-knowledge and an awakening to the knowledge that the world is an illusion.

The phantom world

People were eating heartily at a lunch bhikṣā[1] where Guruji was invited. When dessert was served, one person noticed a basket of ripe fruit on the side table and thought: *Why are they not giving these ripe bananas to Guruji?* He went to the basket and plucked a banana.

It broke.

Everybody laughed.

The whole basket of fruit was made of plastic!

"Guruji, did you know... ?" asked the unfortunate man.

"I was not tempted," chuckled Guruji, "because I knew it was not real."

When does attraction for the world come? It's when there is the false notion that the world is real. The person who thinks the mirage in the desert is water will run towards it. But a

[1]offering of food

person who knows the truth, sees the mirage as an illusion, and will not be attracted to it.

The ever changing world is born out of māyā (illusion) alone. Each person creates his own world around him due to his ignorance. Tamas veils Reality (non-apprehension of Reality); and rajas creates agitations in the mind (or misapprehension of Reality). As a result of a combination of the two, we see things that are not really there – just as when the rope is not recognized as a rope but seen as a snake, or the mirage created by the sun in the desert is seen as water. Sāttvika māyā or vidyā māyā (discrimination of Reality) is the X factor which liberates us from the illusion that the world is real.

Man and
Wiseman

When the knowledge of the Truth has not taken place, the individual identifies with the body-mind-intellect equipment and gives a reality to the world of objects-emotions-thoughts. He reacts to all situations in life and suffers, falsely thinking that it is happening to him.

After gaining the knowledge of the Truth, the Man of Wisdom sees all situations, circumstances, challenges and calamities in life as an illusion and is not disturbed by them. His reaction to these situations is that of a detached observer. When the world lashes out at him, he receives it but never reacts to it. He continues to live in the same world so long as his physical body lingers about him, and responds to the external stimuli with all the instruments of action and perception, exactly like any other man in the world. His uniqueness is not in the cessation of all his activities in the outside world, but in the quality of his heart, wherein there is not a trace of attachment, nor is there any identification with the world. An equanimity and balance of personality can be observed in all his interactions. Thus, he remains established in his supreme wisdom and ever a God-man, he moves among other men.

The heart
of the matter

"What is spirituality?" asked Guruji.

"Doing your duty," replied one man.

"Giving happiness," said another.

"It is selfless service," said a social worker.

"To be good," said one person.

"It is to follow the teachings of the Guru and Scriptures."

"Love is spirituality."

"Being *yourself*," said Guruji.

All methods of self purification, such as selfless service, doing one's duty, listening to the teachings of the Guru, etc. prepare the mind for the higher. And as such, they are sādhanās or spiritual practices, so that we may come to live a spiritual life. However, spirituality is to inquire into the Truth, to be the Truth, to live the Truth.

*To realize the Self is itself the greatest worship that one can offer to the Self. The greatest adoration that we can give to the Supreme, or to a Teacher, is to become **It** – Swami Chinmayananda*

Master
of the mind

On a late afternoon, many families and their children had gathered for an informal satsaṅga with Guruji in Minneapolis, USA.

As he settled in his chair and started talking to each person, a strange squeaky noise was heard above the stairs.

"What is that sound?" Guruji asked.

The 14 year old daughter of the house jumped: "Oh! It's my Pepsi."

"What did you say? *Pepsi?*" asked Guruji.

"Pepsi is my pet," said the girl. "He's hungry. Do you want to see him?"

"Yes!" replied Guruji.

The little girl got Pepsi down and took him out of his pen. Pepsi was a guinea pig. She carried him in her arms and approached Guruji.

"I will do namaskāra[1] from a distance," he said.

[1] greeting

Pepsi was put back in his pen.

"I also have a pet!" exclaimed Guruji.

The children were excited.

"What? Where? Who?" they asked.

Guruji playfully gazed at the children in the room and said: "It is my mind! *My pet is my mind.*"

"My pet is my mind. It is one of a kind," he rhymed. "I take it out when I want, play with it, and keep it back."

The mind has the capacity to run into sense objects at any point through any crack in self-control. Once it escapes, it makes a person the victim of sense pleasures. The seeker should stay the course of viveka (discrimination) and vairāgya (dispassion) in order to master the mind. The mind should be in the pocket of the intellect and not the other way around.

When the mind listens to the intellect, there will be no conflict of purpose between heart and head, ending all agitations in the mind. Such a personality is integrated and able to achieve any goal in life. A purified mind, integrated with the intellect, is the most powerful instrument in creation.

Let a man lift himself by his own self alone, and not allow himself to fall. For this self alone is the friend of oneself, and this self alone is the enemy of oneself. **Bhagavad Gītā, Ch. 6 Verse 5**

Mind alone is the cause of bondage and the means to freedom for the jīva. **Amṛta Bindu Upaniṣad, Mantra 2**

The tricky business
of the mind

All things in the world of plurality, including the thoughts in a human mind, are constantly appearing and disappearing. Nothing can remain the same, not even for a short period, where change alone is the changeless law. Not only is the external world finite, as it has a beginning and an end, but it is also impermanent, meaning, the same object which gives pleasure at one moment becomes the cause of pain at another time. The Man of Wisdom understands the inconsistent, changing nature of all things in the world, including the mind, and does not put his trust in them.

The Self alone is the changeless substratum of all changes. The Self alone is worthy of all trust.

Making lemonade
from lemons

Deciding that he needed to do something to lighten his guilty conscience, the head of the publications department at Central Chinmaya Mission Trust went on a fast. On day two, he was not only guilt-ridden, but also very hungry. He told a friend his story. He had neglected to consult the coordinator of proof-reading, he explained, in order to expedite the printing of an urgent book. The coordinator was very angry, and had asked for a written apology from Guruji.

"What did Guruji do?" asked the friend.

"He sent him a written 'regret note'," said the distressed head of publications, "and he called the coordinator to pacify him".

"So, why are you fasting?"

"It's my fault! Guruji had to apologize because of me!" he cried.

Not quite sure what to make of the situation, the friend went to Guruji.

"Guruji, I thought I should inform you that he is fasting because he feels guilty," he told Guruji. "Today is his second day."

"The coordinator does very good work for the Mission. I can write any number of such apology notes, if the Mission is better served by them!" exclaimed Guruji.

He then made a phone call to the head of publications. "Hari Om!" said Guruji on the phone. "You are coming for lunch, no? I am waiting for you."

One of the most difficult things in life is to say: *I am sorry.* The individual ego comes in the way. However, the Man of Wisdom has no ego; he is a true leader, and has no qualms in saying 'sorry'. His vision rests not on the little ego, but on the greater good. When working in the field, the goal is higher than the individual ego.

Light years
ahead of y'all

Yesterday is the past and tomorrow is the future. Today is a gift, which is why they call it the present.[1]

"Oh Guruji," exclaimed a very important person as he sipped a cup of tea. "How do you see the future?"

"I don't try," said Guruji. "Jo bhī hai, yaha phala hai".[2]

Whatever we are meeting in life in the present moment is the result or prasāda (blessings, fruit) of our own past actions, for the great spiritual law of cause and effect pervades all life. If we manifest friendliness, the world becomes friendly to us. If we manifest hostility, the world responds likewise. The world is like a mirror. What we give comes back to us.

Once it is clearly understood that we receive only what

---

[1]quote by Bill Keane | [2]Whatever is there is the blessing of past actions

we justly deserve, then the attitude with which we meet all present situations, good or bad, will be one of acceptance, where we accept all situations as the blessings or grace of the Lord. And, because of this right attitude, the mind is freed from agitation, thereby making it possible to act well in the present.

A world
without *Me*

The Jai Bharati IV music festival at the Chinmaya Centre of World Understanding in New Delhi was in full swing. Suddenly, the performer for the last day was taken ill and the organisers were left without an artiste.

Guruji decided that the gap would be filled up by 'in-house' talent, starting with himself and followed by four others. A notice was prepared to inform all about the change. It read:

> In the auspicious presence of H.H. Swami Tejomayananda, Head of Chinmaya Mission Worldwide, the program for the next day will have performances by Pramodini and Chittaranjan Rao (vocal, tabla) followed by Lalit and Satish Kumar (sitar, tabla).

A draft printout of the notice was shown to Guruji for his approval.

Looking at it, he pulled a face. "I am also going to sing, no?" he said. "Who made this?"

"I did, Guruji," said one girl.

"If everything is happening without me," he said looking at her, "then, *who am I?*"

The girl left to change the notice to: *Led by Swami Tejomayananda...*

Guruji smiled. "She doesn't know I am quoting a dialogue from the Aitareya Upaniṣad," he said to the remaining onlookers. "In it, the Lord has a question: 'Who am I? If the entire saṅgata[1] is happening without me, then *why am I here?*'"

Aitareya Upaniṣad: The Self thought: 'How can this be without me? If speaking is done by speech, breathing by breath, seeing by the eyes, hearing by the ears, smelling by the nose and thinking by the mind, then who am I?' **Mantra 1.3.11**

A house is not built for the dignity of the pillar or the strength of the walls, or the protection of the beams or the preservation of the floor. It is made to house the master, who is an independent entity, who can at his will, walk out of the assemblage or walk in as he pleases. Without a 'Knowing Principle', or the Master, there can be no unified

[1]assemblage of body-mind-intellect and so on

or synchronized experience throughout the assemblage. Similarly, the saṅgata cannot have any justification or fulfilment without the Self or the Master. Without this 'Knowing Principle', the saṅgata has no existence of its own.

Mirror, mirror on the wall,
who's the changeless of us all?

Ātman is the Self – all pervading, ever present, the Eternal Principle of Life.

Jīva, or the sense of individuality, is the Self reflected in the equipment of the mind. In this example, just as without the woman, there can be no reflection of her; so too, without the Self, there can be no reflected Self or Jīva. The reflection will exist as long as the mirror exists. So too, the Jīva, or the limited individual, exists as long as the mind functions.

Though the reflected image is of the same form as the object reflected, there is a lateral inversion of details in the reflection. The left arm of the woman will be seen as the right side of her own reflection. This 'lateral inversion' of our true Self in the mind, as the limited individual, is the cause of confusions and sorrows in life, saṁsāra.

Also, if the mirror crashes, only the reflection ends and not the object that is being reflected. So too, when the mind ends, the Jīva or the limited individuality alone ends, not the Self, the Ātman. And after a long span of existence as a limited individuality, which is a painful distortion of our true personality, when this limitation comes to an end, it is a most welcome awakening.

The earth, moon and
the vocabulary of knowledge

Everyone in the camp was discussing the meaning of *knowledge*, as used in 'Self-knowledge'. It was generally admitted to be all too confusing. If knowledge was not intellectual knowledge, and intellectual knowledge was the only knowledge the intellect knew, then how was the intellect to know knowledge, which was not intellectual knowledge in the first place?

"Guruji, this term *knowledge,*" opined one intellectual, whose words were usually considered weighty, "I don't understand it at all!"

"Tell me, when you look straight ahead," said Guruji, pointing to the road in front of them, "do you see Earth as round or flat?"

"Flat," replied the smart man.

"Now tell me," continued Guruji, "why do you know that Earth is round?"

"Because, the scientists have proved it," said the man. "I believe them."

"Ok. You have *faith* in the scientists," said Guruji. "Your knowledge is intellectual or book knowledge, since it is based on a person or a text book."

"But suppose you were put on a space ship and sent to the moon," continued Guruji. "From the moon, you saw the whole Earth, and because of your own *direct experience* you saw that Earth was round. Now, when you come back to Earth, let us suppose, the scientists changed their minds and claimed that Earth is octave. Would you believe them?"

"No!" exclaimed the man.

"Why?" asked Guruji.

"Because I saw Earth for myself, and it was round!"

"Exactly!" smiled Guruji. "Your intellectual knowledge is based on *faith* in a textbook, a Scripture or a Teacher. But once you have had a *direct experience,* the knowledge is no longer intellectual, it becomes a crystal-clear conviction. Even if the scientists change their minds, you will not!"

"Remember, you do not have to remain on Moon to know that Earth is round. Even if you come back to Earth, and again see it as flat, you will always know that it is round, because of your direct experience," said Guruji. "Once the knowledge of the Truth takes place, you do not have to be in a state of samādhi[1] or experience at all times to be a jīvanamukta.[2] Even when the experience of samādhi goes away, the knowledge of the Truth remains."

"Ok. Now suppose, when you were on the moon, you think what you see is Jupiter, and not Earth. What happens?"

"I don't know," said the man. "What happens?"

"Nothing happens! If you do not have the right knowledge, the experience is useless! If you wrongly think the round planet is Jupiter, then your knowledge is incomplete and ineffectual, even though you had the right experience. This is why the Scriptures give importance to *knowledge* and not just *experience*."

Intellectual knowledge of the Self without the actual experience is ineffectual. So also, experience without knowledge is ineffectual. We have to experience the Self and also know the Self's true nature. The Mahāvākyas[3] which expound the central teaching of the Scriptures reveal the identity of the Self as Brahman. With this knowledge, when we experience the Self, samsāra or the realm of bondage comes to an end.

The experience of the Self as the infinite Brahman is

[1]absorption of mind in the *I am Brahman* thought | [2]one who is liberated while living | [3]statements from Upaniṣad revealing the identity of the Self with the supreme Brahman

not a mediate experience; meaning it is not gained through the instrument of any equipment. However, the Teacher, Scriptures, sādhanā (spiritual practice) and study, all help the mind to withdraw from its preoccupations with the outside world. Because the Infinite is our essential nature, the withdrawn mind, held in attention with full alertness, can receive intimations from the Infinite. Such a contemplative mind develops intuitive power by which it comes to apprehend Reality. It is an *im*mediate (without mediation, direct) experience.

When knowledge metamorphosis into wisdom, it seems to be empowered with an almost miraculous loftiness. Such wisdom turns into an all-encompassing glow of intuition. Everything becomes revealed, everything becomes understood instantaneously. *Intuition* replaces knowledge, *knowing* turns into *being,* and life becomes infused with *wisdom.*

The night has
a thousand eyes

A group of pilgrims decided to include a visit to Guruji in their itinerary. After staying a week, they were overcome with wonder and staggered by the reflected glory of Chinmaya Vibhooti.

On the last night, everyone gathered around Guruji in the car park under a star-studded sky.

"What will you remember most when you leave from here?" Guruji asked everyone.

"This place, it is so impressive," said one person.

"Gurudev's life-like wax statue," said another.

"I will remember your morning talks, Guruji," said one lady.

"They explained everything in such a simple manner."

Guruji looked questioningly at others.

"I am going to miss everyone."

"Guruji, it is the vibrations here."

"Chinmaya Jeevan Darshan was the highlight of my trip!"

"I think I will remember your jokes, Guruji."

The evening ended and Guruji started to walk back to his kuṭiyā.

A little girl ran to Guruji and motioned for him to bend. She then whispered in his ear: "I will remember *YOU*".

Guruji smiled, and whispered back in her ear: "Actually, you have said the correct thing".

How often do we remember God? More often, we remember everything else but God. Even on a pilgrimage, we remember the journey and its events more than we remember God. In life, we remember everything we have been given by God, but we don't remember Him.

This is because we don't have our priorities right. When we have a chance to be in the proximity of a living Master, we do not value him for the right reason, which is the knowledge of the Truth. We give emphasis to people and things around him, but not to *Him*.

Unless we have our priorities right, we will not receive

the full effect, or grace of the Master. And, our priorities are guided by our vāsanās (desires). The values that we uphold in life will determine our priorities in life.

Reality is everyone's property. Therefore it is said: *Ask and it shall be given, for it is yours by birthright.* The tragedy of this world is that no one asks. They ask for what they can see – passing unrealities. No one realizes the worth and value of that which cannot be seen. There is no lack of *THAT* which we are seeking. But, there is a lack in the seeking.

The magical
charm of the pied piper

A newcomer wanted to establish if Guruji was a genuinely holy man.

"Have you got any siddhis,"[1] he asked him point blank.

"What do you mean by siddhis?" replied Guruji

"Like floating in the air or walking on water and all that," enlightened the man.

"Oh! That! Yes! Yes! Of course I can walk on water!"

"Really? Can you demonstrate?" continued the man.

"Of course!"

And Guruji went to the bathroom, poured a bucket of water on the floor and walked up and down on it.

Many genuine spiritual seekers are waylaid on the path to the Truth by the lure of mystical powers. To approach a Man of

[1]mystical powers

Wisdom for any reason other than to gain the knowledge of the Absolute Truth is a sheer waste of opportunity.

In **Kaṭhopaniṣad,** *Naciketas tells the Lord of Death: All these pleasures pass away, O End of all! They weaken the power of life. And indeed how short is all life! Keep thy horses and dancing and singing. Grant me the gift that unveils the mystery of the Self. This is the only gift that Naciketas can ask.* **Mantra 1.1.26**

Why pray?

The mind must also be cleaned everyday through prayer. Just as a pot with glue in it is called a glue pot; and if you take out the glue and put ink in it, it is called an ink pot. So also, a mind with angry thoughts is called an angry mind; with pure thoughts, it's called a pure mind.

Depending upon the thoughts that fill it, the mind becomes good or bad, pure or impure. As the thoughts, so the mind; as the mind, so the man. Whilst the body needs a bath each day to keep it clean; similarly, the mind needs to be cleaned regularly through prayer.

The homecoming

Duty is an altogether wobbly word used in present-day language with limitless possibilities for compromise.

An elderly lady, who wanted to impress upon her children the importance of duty, came to Guruji.

"Guruji, please guide these youngsters as to what is their duty," she said.

"Ammā,[1] whether you are young or old, adult or child, everyone has only one duty. Come Home," answered Guruji.

"Huh?"

Not everyone grasped the implication of what Guruji had said.

Still, one youngster asked: "How?"

"Remember God."

[1] lady in general, often an elderly lady

Everyone wants happiness. Whether we understand it or not, every action of ours is in the pursuit of happiness; for we are subconsciously guided by our essential nature, which is happiness (bliss) to return home to its true nature. Thus, the only duty (or dharma) in life is this homecoming to the Self, to God.

Abandoning all dharmas (of body, mind and intellect), take refuge in Me alone; I will liberate you from the bondage of all sins. Grieve not. **Bhagavad Gītā Ch. 18 Verse 66**

How? By remembering who we are. We cannot become something which we already eternally are. The realization of the Truth is not the result of action, for if anything is the result of action, it means there was a time when it did not exist and has since come into being. Butter does not have to do anything to be soft. Ice will be cold. Fire will burn and be hot. It is their nature. Yet, the simple fact is that without the right effort to remember God (sādhanā), Self-Realization is impossible. Sādhana removes the veil of ignorance that prevents the Self from being recognized.

The length of
your *love* line

Guruji was on one of his many train journeys, travelling to Pathankot in the company of many ācāryas, devotees and disciples. He started asking everyone who their Iṣṭa Devatā[1] was.

All had something to say.

"Kṛṣṇa!"

"Rāma!"

"Śiva!"

"Devī!"

One sweet elderly lady said: "All are equally worshipful to me".

"What!" exclaimed Guruji. "How can that be? I may think of all women as my mothers, but I know who my real mother is."

"If we want to increase our love for the Lord," he added,

---

[1]chosen form of God for worship

"then we must *cultivate* a relationship with Him".

Devotion or love for God is developed by nurturing a bond with God. When there is a relationship with God – be it as a Guru, father, brother, friend, etc. – it becomes easier and more natural to remember Him and his glories. King Daśaratha saw the Lord as his son. Bharata saw Him as a brother. Sudāmā saw him as a friend and the gopīs as their beloved. Whoever be the Iṣṭa and whatever the relationship with Him, the important point is that in order for love to grow, it must be cultivated.

The practical method of cultivating such a relationship is prayer, keeping a special time for the Lord during the day for prayer. When the seeker pours himself out in love for the Lord of his heart; the more he pours himself out, the more his love increases. Love and labour go hand in hand. Where there is love, labour becomes a joy. The very goal to be reached is Love and the way to reach it is also by love. Thus, in devotion, divine love is both the means and the goal. By cultivating love, the lover identifies with the beloved. There is no 'I' separate from Him.

Thank God
you're here!

God's gifts put man's best dreams to shame. We seldom count the gifts of the Lord. He is continuously giving and is never tired of giving. Yet, how often do we recognize His bounties? In the Bhagavad Gītā, Lord Kṛṣṇa beautifully dramatises: *I am the vitality in the sun, the fertility in the soil, the nourishment in plants and the food that nourishes. I make digestion happen, and with Me come memory and wisdom, and without Me they depart.* **Bhagavad Gītā, Ch. 15 Verses 14 & 15**

Two men stood behind prison bars. One saw mud, the other saw stars. If we can recognize how much we have been given, instead of only seeing what we do not have; that in itself will make us a king of kings. Indeed, a king who does not recognise his own status remains a beggar.

Well wisher
or wish fulfiller

"If God answers all sincere prayers," said one person, "then why does he not listen to a mother's prayers for her sick child?"

"This is not true. God is not a wish fulfiller, He is our wisher," replied Guruji. "God answers prayers by giving us what *He* wants, not what *we* want."

"If there are two people praying for the exact same thing, whose wish should be answered? A potter and a farmer both pray to God. The potter asks for sunshine to dry his pots, and the farmer asks for rain for his harvest. Whose wish should be fulfilled?"

"How can we decide what is best for the child? *God alone knows what is best.*"

Nowhere in the entire range of religious scriptures of any religion does it ever say that if we pray to God, everything will turn out as we want. Any sincere prayer implies a quality of faith in God that makes the heart firmly trust and believe in God's wisdom and goodness, despite all the painful and distressing situations that may be happening.

I am the Way, and the Master who watches in silence; thy friend and thy shelter and thy abode of peace. **Bhagavad Gītā, Ch. 9 Verse 18**

The Infinite is a friend of the finite, whose only anxiety is for the security and the well being of the befriended – Swami Chinmayananda

Head or
heart: At wit's end

"Which is it, Guruji?" asked one person. "Should decisions be based on emotions or the intellect?"

"The question is strange," remarked Guruji. "Decisions should be based on neither! They should only be based on dharma." [1]

"When Lord Rāma was to leave for the forest, he was told by his mother: *Obedience to the mother comes before obedience to the father. I order you not to go.* Lord Rāma agreed that the mother comes before the father, but in this case, her decision was wrong because her argument was based on her love for Lord Rāma and not on dharma."

"King Daśaratha ordered the chariot that was leaving with Lord Rāma to stop: *As a king, I command you to stop.* But Lord Rāma instructed the charioteer to ignore the command saying: *On your return, if questioned, you tell the king that you did not hear.*"

"It is not that Lord Rāma wanted to promote a lie. But

[1] nature of a thing, duty

since King Daśaratha was using his position as a king to appease his heart, the decision was wrong."

"Even King Daśaratha, much as he wished for Lord Rāma not to leave for the forest, carried out the promise given to Kaikeyī because it was his dharma to fulfil a promise once given. In fact, he hoped that Lord Rāma would be disobedient for once, and refuse to go! But Lord Rāma is the epitome of dharma."

"Decisions should be based on dharma, always."

Dharma can be understood in three ways.

Dharma means the nature or characteristic of a thing, without which the thing ceases to be that thing. For example: the sweetness of sugar, the heat of fire, the coolness of water, and Existence-Consciousness-Bliss in the human being. To abide in one's true nature is dharma.

Dharma also means one's own inherent aptitude or svadharma. For example, if a young boy is gifted in music and gets fulfilment by being a musician, then it is his dharma to choose the path that truly helps his self-unfoldment. He then ought to become a musician, and not choose to become, say, a businessman, which might give him more money but also more agitation, as his inherent nature is not in sync with business life.

And, dharma means the performance of one's duties. Each one of us has duties which come to us unasked, depending on the status, position, place or situation we are in. For example, a student's duty is to study; an army man's duty is to defend the country. To do one's duty is dharma.

Thus, dharma is righteous action. It is to do what is right, based on the scriptural teaching, the wisdom of the wise and one's own inner voice. All these three are compasses that help in determining the right course of action.

The individual should decide his dharma in any given situation in life with a calm and serene mind, without prejudice or favour. The observance of dharma fulfils two objectives: happiness in life and liberation from bondage.

Standpoint
of dharma

The dharma[1] of an individual, suggested by *where he sits,* is the duty required by him according to his station in life, *where he stands.* In the Bhagavad Gītā, Lord Kṛṣṇa tells Arjuna that his dharma is to fight the war as a warrior and a protector of his people.

Sometimes, there can be a conflict in one's station in life. For example, Arjuna was in conflict over his dharma to protect his people, and also his dharma towards his relatives – to not wage war on them. In such situations, dharma must be dictated by the larger good or benefit to the largest number, ahead of one's own individual benefit. Thus, Lord Kṛṣṇa told Arjuna that his dharma was to fight the war to protect the decaying values in society.

Lord Rāma could have made his father happy by refusing to go to the forest. The vast population of Ayodhya too would have been happy had he not done so. Yet, he choose to go, since it was his dharma in the long term interest of humanity, to not set a precedence of taking back a promise once given, which would have been followed down the ages. Personal sacrifice for the sake of the majority is the principle of all dharma.

The highest dharma of an individual is to attain the Self within, his true nature, wherein the greater and individual good are both served. However, this essential dharma can

[1]nature of a thing, duty

67

only be lived once the individual renounces his ego; that is, gives up his non-essential dharmas of the body-mind-intellect. Only then can the individual express his divine status as the all pervading Self. To live truly as the Self, and to express its infinite perfection through all our actions and in all our contacts with the outer world is to rediscover dharma.

Time tested and
fool proof

Guruji was standing at the train station one day. Holding his Rāmāyaṇa in one hand, he was waiting for the train, when a young passer-by with his wife and child came up to him and said:

"What is the need to study the Rāmāyaṇa and stuff like this? It is the twenty first century, in case you haven't noticed!"

"You are right," said Guruji.

The train arrived. The young man jumped into the crowded train, and just then, the train started to move. His wife and child were left behind on the platform. The wife started to wail and the young man could be heard shouting curses at the Indian railway system.

"You see," said Guruji, "if you had studied the Rāmāyaṇa, you would have known that as a husband, you take care of your wife and child first. And only then you jump into the train!"

The teachings in the Scriptures are timeless, ever fresh. They prescribe time-tested methods for happy living and the path to Godhood. As such, they are a way of life and are never out of date.

Love's loopy
logic

The younger generation, as we all know, comes from a place of sound logic where fruit is fruit, a spade is called a spade, and *love* is open-ended; it can be a comma, a question mark, or an exclamation point in life.

One day, Guruji had been invited for bhikṣā,[1] when the man of the house took him aside and said:

"Guruji, my son is very rebellious. I want him to have the upanayanam[2] ceremony and he is refusing to have it done. I don't know what to do."

Guruji promised to talk to his son.

After the bhikṣā, the boy was driving Guruji back to the ashram. Guruji brought up the subject of the upanayanam.

The boy flared up. "I don't believe in all this superstition. *Why* should I get it done? There is no use, no benefit! It makes no sense!"

Guruji had noticed the boy was a smoker. "You smoke

[1]offering of food | [2]thread ceremony

cigarettes?" he asked him.

"Yes," the boy admitted.

"Why did you start smoking?"

"All my friends do it."

"When they asked you to join them, did you question *why* you should smoke?" asked Guruji. "Did you stop to examine the logic of it? Did you weigh the pros and cons?"

The boy was silent.

"Why do you ask these questions now? If you can take up smoking without questioning, why argue so much over an upanayanam which can do you no harm. And think of how much joy it will give your father!"

It worked! The boy had his upanayanam ceremony done.

It costs a person nothing, not even the compromising of an ideal (or conviction), to make another person happy. In turn, we receive the joy of making another happy. Then why be so stingy with a selfless act?

Also, we often arrive at false convictions without a proper enquiry, simply because 'everybody else is doing it'.

The omission
commission

One day, Brahmacārī Vivek Chaitanya went for bhikṣā.[1] He was served a wonderful meal by the lady of the house, at the end of which her husband declared: "Brahmacārīji, I never come for your classes".

What could the poor brahmacārī reply.

"Ask me why I don't come."

"Why don't you come?" asked the brahmacārī.

"Because," he continued, quite pleased with himself, "my friend, who works in the same office as me, comes to your classes. And, I don't know what you have taught him, but he comes to the office and tells me: *I am going to meditate; you please take care of my files.* He sits in his chair chanting OM, and I have to do all his work! That's why."

"That's fine," laughed the brahmacārī. "But when the salary comes, you take his salary as well, and tell him to keep meditating."

[1]offering of food

The mind should be where the hands are working. The office is not a place to meditate! Escaping from our duty in life in the name of spirituality is not true spirituality. Rather, dedicated performance to one's duty is a spiritual discipline of a very high order.

Not by refraining from action does a man attain freedom from action. Not by mere renunciation does he attain supreme perfection. **Bhagavad Gītā, Ch. 3 Verse 4**

Also, the fruit of action depends on the action, as per the law of cause and effect. As you sow, so shall you reap.

Hey!
Look around you

The very characteristics of the Man of Wisdom become spiritual practices for the seeker. The Man of Wisdom lives in a sense of oneness with the whole cosmos and considers the welfare of others before his own.

In the day-to-day interactions with the world in which the seeker is living, he must be fully aware of the needs and sorrows of all around him, and must seek to find within himself a kindness and tolerance, such, that it makes his heart melt for the sorrow of others.

The spirit of sacrifice and the capacity to find within oneself enough sympathy to serve others, thus putting their welfare first, is one of the most important qualities in a true seeker. While serving, it is important: 1) to keep the Nārāyaṇa bhāva that *I am serving the Lord* 2) not to demand the fruits of the service, and 3) to renounce the sense of doer-ship, that *I am serving.* The attitude should be: *The Lord is serving through me.*

In Kaṭhopaniṣad, Naciketas did not come to the final question seeking his own liberation, until he had first fulfilled his obligations to his father and to society at large. The spirit of service and sacrifice is an unavoidable qualification for a true seeker, who wants to gain success in his pursuit of the Truth.

The altered ego

A religious minded person returned to the matter of Scripture. He did not understand how he was supposed to practically function in the world without an ego.[1]

"How can I work if I give up my identity?" he questioned Guruji.

"When you are with yourself, remember so'ham.[2]

When you are at work outside, remember daso'ham".[3]

At the time of contemplation, the thought process to remove the ego and identify with Brahman should be: *I am Brahman.* However, in our interaction with the world, there are two approaches to remove the ego. The first is: *God is working through me.* And if this is difficult; then the second approach should be: *I am working for God.*

[1]sense of limited 'I' | [2]I am *That* | [3]I am His servant

The luggage
of life

When preparing to travel, lay out all your clothes and all your money. Then take half the clothes and twice the money.[1] Ordinarily, it would be sound advice, but what of a sannyāsi?[2]

"Guruji, please do not say no," said a lady. "I have bought you a gift. It is a luggage bag. All your clothes will fit in it very well." She wheeled in a bag.

Guruji took the bag, but asked the lady to come inside his room. Opening his old bag, he started to transfer everything into the new one. After he had emptied everything, he handed the old bag to the lady.

"A sannyāsi should only have one," he said.

After a brief pause, he added: "In truth, real sannyāsa[3] is inner, and it is a must for everybody".

[1]quote by Susan Heller | [2]man of renunciation | [3]path of renunciation

The practical aspect of renunciation of desires is pointed out by suggesting that we should keep no extra *(only have one)* other than what we need for our day to day functions.

However, the true essence of renunciation (indicated by real sannyāsa) is in giving up the attachments (desires) in the mind. Real sannyāsa is equivalent to true vairāgya (detachment), where not only is there detachment from external objects and circumstances, but it is the mental condition in which the mind no longer runs after the phenomenal world in the hope of gaining peace and joy.

Kurdle
the choice

A large business house asked the ācārya of Sandeepany Sadhanalaya, Powai, to speak on the death anniversary of their family member. The ācārya could not speak in Marāṭhī, so he sent his student, Sudhakar,[1] in his place.

On the day of the gathering, the young Sudhakar was seated right in the front of a crowd of 2000 people, in a place of honour with other venerable speakers. Looking no more than a lad in his early 20s, the organiser was concerned about the little brahmacārī's public speaking abilities.

"Can the fellow speak?" he asked the Mission member who had escorted him.

"I think so!" was the reply.

Before long, Sudhakar was called on the dais.

He started to tell a story of a man who would only eat curd and not any other milk product. The Mission member gave him a nervous glance from the audience.

[1]name given to Guruji by his parents

"This man would only eat curd," continued the brahmacārī, "not any other milk product. When people asked him why he would only eat curd, the man would say: 'I will get milk in any birth, whether a cat, dog or buffalo, but curd I will only get in a human birth'."

Naming the departed family member, he said: "... He lived up to the dignity and responsibility of a human birth. To eat, sleep and die is the prerogative of animals, but to serve people, as he served you, only in a human life is this opportunity given. He chose to do sevā,[2] which is why so many of you have gathered in his memory here today."

Sudhakar's speech has not been forgotten by those who were present at the ceremony that day.

Discrimination is the prerogative of the human intellect, and for all living creatures a human birth is indeed rare. To be born as a human being is a sign of the Lord's grace. Then, to employ deep discriminative understanding in life, and to recognize the ultimate futility of ordinary selfish pursuits of life, is rarer still. Only the very rare choose to pursue a life of service; when in fact, selfless service is a joyful way to put our life to use, and one of the easiest methods of self-purification on the spiritual path.

[2]service to others

The philosophy
of chen and ṭana ṭana

In February 2010, on a beautiful spring afternoon in Ādi
Śaṅkara Nilayam, Veliyanad, a fascinating conversation took
place. One gentleman from the south had a typically strong
accent and was explaining that Chinmaya Mission, Kannur,
had adopted ten children from Kargil after the war.

"Chen children," he said.

"How many?" asked a lady.

"Chen children... " he replied.

"You said ten?"

"Chen... seven Muslims, three Buddhists... chen
children."

"How many?" she said again. "Is it seven children or
three children?"

"Chen," he said.

"Now now... that's three plus seven... chen," clarified
another.

"Kisakā bhāgya unheṁ kahāṁ le jātā hai,"[1] said Guruji.

"We are doing so much good work," said yet another. "See the work of CORD,[2] then these ten children, everywhere we are doing so much charity. But nobody knows! Guruji, we should publicise all this."

"Why?" replied Guruji. "Those who need to know – know. The person who has done the charity knows; the person for whom you are doing the charity, knows. And God knows! What is the need for anybody else to know? Aba hamem apanā ṭana ṭana thoṛī na bajānā hai!"[3]

The song of success sung by the ego ever hums in the heart of a materialist. Under the spell of its lullaby, the higher instincts and divine yearnings in man go into a sleep of intoxication. The highest form of renunciation is the renunciation of the ego. Name and fame must also be ultimately renounced, if one is to attain liberation.

*When man is able to temporarily overcome his baser tendencies, he develops an ego that **he** did it, forgetting that it was Nārāyaṇa's grace that made it happen – Swami Chinmayananda*

[1]Look where destiny takes each one of us | [2]Chinmaya Organization for Rural Development | [3]Where is the need to blow our own trumpet!

Easy come, easy go

Renunciation does not mean that we literally give up the object, emotion or thought. True renunciation is non-attachment in the mind, where the mind is not dependent on objects or emotions, and remains unaffected in their absence.

The practice of renunciation is meant for the purpose of developing an attitude of detachment. Such a mind is not dependent on the world for its happiness and can immediately drop the attachment to the object or emotion if needed, in the event that it is unavailable at some point in the future.

No*thing* of value

Guruji would often sit on the floor in his kuṭiyā in Chinmaya Vibhooti, Kolwan, playing on the 'shortened' harmonium, a judicious instrument that had been especially made to suit his voice. The lower and higher keys had been sensibly removed, since he did not use them. "My voice does not go there," he would say.

One day, while he sang many melodious bhajanas, a crowd started to gather. One and all, they sat down around him in silence. As time went by, the atmosphere in the room became noticeably elevated and when he finished, everybody was speechless.

Guruji saw the expressions and quietly said: "We don't need any*thing* to be happy".

Happiness is the true nature of the eternal Self. Desires for things of the world create clouds of agitation in the mind, which reflect as passing shadows. When we let go of our desire for things of the world; the eternal Self shines through unobstructed in all its resplendence, expressing its true nature – which is happiness.

Whenever the mind is quietened, a ray of the Infinite bliss shines through – Swami Chinmayananda

Restlessness
on the run

Deciding, for once, that the entire family must spend a week at a spiritual camp in Sidhbari, the parents of one teenage city boy *made* their son come to the ashram. Two days of ashram food and routine, and the teenager began a chant of his own.

"I want to go back! I want to go back!" was his constant refrain from morning to noon, dusk to nightfall.

"Don't you see the snow clad mountains?" asked the father.

"No!"

"Haven't you made any friends?" cajoled the mother.

"No! I want to go back!"

At last the parents relented and said: "Go and ask for permission from Guruji. If he grants it, you may go back."

Guruji had seen the boy grow up and knew the family well. After listening to a lengthy tirade from the boy, he asked him one simple question.

"What will you do there?"

"Nothing," said the boy for lack of a well thought out answer.

"Nothing!" remarked Guruji. "Then you better *do* that here."

We are restless because we have not resigned ourselves to the teaching that we do not have to *do* anything to *be* (happy, enlightened). Just as silence is present in the midst of sound, which is only superimposed over it; the Truth is present in the midst of untruth. We do not have to move one foot to reach it. We only have to stop disturbing it, stop bringing in something else.

Why did God
create the world?

There is one question which every young person asks his parents. And parents think it is a very intelligent question.

"Guruji, you know, my son asked me a very intelligent spiritual question." She poked her son. "Betā,[1] ask Guruji! Ask na! Go on! Ask your question to Guruji!"

"Guruji, why did God create this world?" the son asked.

"How do you know there is a God and that God is the creator of the world?" asked Guruji in return.

"I have heard it in the scriptures."

"So you accept the scriptures?"

"Yes."

"Fully?"

"Fully."

"Scriptures say that you are God. So now, *you* tell *me,* why

[1]son

did *you* create this world?"

The question is a logical absurdity. God is omnipotent. Hence to ask why he did this or that is to limit him. It implies that God needed a reason or a purpose to create the world, which in turn suggests that there is a result that God wants, which exists, but is not in His hands! By logic, this negates the entire definition of an infinite omnipotent God.

Moreover, this question can only arise from the standpoint of the ignorant jīva (individual ego) who gives a reality to creation. From the standpoint of God, there is no creation, it does not exist! If it is seen by us, then it is an illusion, a passing unreality.

This world of objects and the sense of individuality is the gross manifestation of the ego (sense of limited 'I'), and is the untruth, an illusion. In the Rāma Gītā, Lord Rāma explains to Lakṣmaṇa that ignorance manifests in the form of the ego which says *I and mine, you and yours; and this is māyā (illusion)*. The ego projects this sense of separation and limits itself to a finite body. Thus, the ego creates the illusion of an entire world of separate objects and bodies in the mind of an individual.

The ṛṣis have clearly pointed to the One Truth, the One Absolute Reality and said there is nothing other than it. There cannot be any other object created within the One, when the definition itself suggests there is no duality.

Sense
and sensibility

All good intentions remain in the imagination, unless they are supported by right actions. Grand ideas must be practically implemented, if they are to become an actuality.

Very often, people have a habit of making suggestions from the outside. But unless and until the individual is willing to participate in the suggested change, merely voicing an opinion is often a derogatory exercise, especially if the individual is also not fully informed concerning the said situation.

A matter
of time and place

In his younger days, Brahmacārī Vivek Chaitanya[1] took the bus when he went to take a class. Clinging to a copy of the holy Gītā in one hand, and hanging on to the overhead rod with the other, he would somehow stay on his feet in the crowded bus, as it bumped around on the windy road.

Once, a man standing next to him was curiously staring away.

"Do you study the Gītā?" he asked.

Just then, the bus driver blasted the horn and went over a giant speed breaker at break-neck specd.

"What?" the brahmacārī managed to say in a thin voice.

"Do you study the Gītā?"

"Yes."

The bus took a mammoth swerve. The curious man fell backwards, then straightened himself and continued undeterred.

[1]Guruji's name as a brahmacārī

"What is said in the Gītā?"

"Tadviddhi praṇipātena paripraśnena sevayā![2] Such questions are not to be answered in a moving bus!"

Spirituality is not something that we can start discussing to pass away an idle hour. It is to be understood in an atmosphere of peace and tranquillity; for this understanding is an attempt at comprehending the deep experiences of the Master, expressed not so much through his words, as perhaps through the ring of sincerity that the words carry, when they come from the purity of an established Self. Therefore it is said, that a Guru must be approached with reverence and surrender, then alone can such subtle knowledge be received.

[2]*Know that by long prostration, by question, and service, the wise who have realized the Truth will instruct you in (that) Knowledge.* **Bhagavad Gītā, Ch. 4 Verse 34**

Essay

on a cow

At the end of a three day empowerment conference in Chinmaya International Foundation, one person who had not been in attendance, mischievously asked Guruji: "Were the speakers any good?"

"Three were very good," replied Guruji. "The others did an *Essay on a cow!*"

"Huh? What's that?"

"You don't know!" laughed Guruji. "A boy wrote an essay on a cow for his school homework. That was the only essay he knew how to write. One summer holiday, he went to stay with an uncle outside the city. When he returned back to school, the teacher asked all the children to write an essay on their summer vacation. The boy, who only knew the one essay, wrote: *I went to stay with my uncle in his farm for my summer holidays. My uncle had a cow.* Then he wrote his Essay on a cow, word for word."

"If you always do what you always did," he continued, "then you will always get what you always got. God has a rule: *Use it or lose it!* If you do not use your intellect, you will lose it."

Progress and success are achieved when action is supported with discriminative thinking by the intellect. Blind action alone will only yield limited results. A constant desire and an attempt to better ourselves is the secret of success.

A few
good men

A woman had heard that Guruji was very wise. She persuaded her relatives to make a trip with her to meet him. As the time for the visit grew nearer, it started to rain, and one by one all the relatives dropped out.

The woman was not deterred. She wrote down the address and took a three wheeler to the Mission centre where Guruji was staying.

Once she had met Guruji and introduced herself, she narrated the story of her missing relatives, telling him that many had decided to come, but for one reason or another had changed their minds.

Guruji smiled and said: "Saba kā bulāvā nahīṁ ātā!"[1]

The call of God is not the result of some immediate past action(s) that can be recalled. It comes only to those who have lived for a time respecting dharma.[2] It is the outcome of the

[1]Not everyone gets a calling | [2]duty

evolution and growth of the individual, through moral and ethical living; whereby, the individual has directed himself towards a spiritual life, and therefore the subsequent calling into this path.

Manhood, burning desire for liberation, the capacity to surrender completely to a Man of Wisdom; these three things are rare indeed, and wherever they are found, they are due to the Lord's own Grace. **Vivekacūḍāmaṇī, Verse 3**

This kind of perfect liberation cannot be had without earned merits of a hundred crore lives lived intelligently. **Vivekacūḍāmaṇī, Verse 2**

A leap of
faith

One day, Guruji proposed a question. "How do you make up a riddle?" he asked.

Everyone gave up.

"Start with the answer," he said.

To solve any problem or answer any question, it is first necessary to believe that an answer does in fact exist. Even science must postulate a theory, before it begins to prove it. Similarly, for any philosophical or spiritual progress into the nature of existence, or God, the spiritual seeker must first have the faith in the existence of God. Without faith there can be no real progress. It would effectively be floundering in the dark, not knowing in which direction we are headed. *Faith is the belief in what we do not know, so that we come to know what we believe in.*

Mind your
business!

Once the seeker has outlined a path of austerity – be it in the environment of a spiritual camp in the mountains or at home – he should keep his mind focused on the higher goal he has set for himself, and not get side tracked by outside disturbances.

Rather, any inconveniences or disturbances should be looked upon with acceptance and as a test of endurance.

Titikṣā is the capacity to endure all sorrow and sufferings without struggling for redress or revenge, being always free from anxiety or lament over them. **Vivekacūḍāmaṇī, Verse 24**

Lock, stock
and all smoking barrels

Sitting on the steps in Sandeepany Sadhanalaya, Powai, a sincere seeker was overcome with helplessness. She had done all that she could, and decided that the only alternative left was to 'hand over' all to Guru and God. After all, the Scriptures are full of stories of great devotees who had surrendered themselves to the Lord and had gained everlasting peace and tranquillity. The decision being made, she went to Guruji.

"Guruji, is it not possible for a person to hand over charge of their life to someone else?" she asked.

"One has to take charge of one's own life," he said. "Nobody can live it for you."

Handing over charge of one's life without giving up the attachment to the fruit of action, or because we are unable to cope with the fruit of action, is not surrender. The true spirit of surrender must go hand in hand with acceptance: *It is His will.* Surrender does not put an end to or eliminate activity. But it is no longer ego-directed, or desire directed activity. Surrender is God-governed, God-directed activity; where the *doer-ship* belongs to God and the *doing* is done through the individual.

Creators, leaders
and producers

A wizened businesswoman, who had been attending study classes and running a garment design concern for many years, suddenly developed a strong sense of vairāgya.[1] She decided to close down the entire business and dedicate herself to spiritual life, since she did not need the extra money from her work. Energised with her decision, she informed Guruji when he next came to her city.

"Why?" he demanded.

The lady was taken by surprise, and gave no answer.

"Tell me," he asked, "are you not gifted with the power to create?"

The lady nodded.

"Use the gift God has given you. Each of us has a different gift, and we must do the best with what we have been given."

"How many households are sustained by your

[1] dispassion

company?" asked Guruji.

"A few hundred," replied the lady.

"The extra money may not mean much to you, but it would be life changing for your workers. What will they do? Work for them, since they need your talent, and give your extra money to others if you have enough. *The creators in this world are few, and the imitators are many. The leaders in the world are few, and the followers are many. The producers in the world are few, and the consumers are many.*"

One need not leave one's home, family or profession in order to lead a spiritual life. What has to be left is the ego, the wrong idea that I am so and so and that I am the doer. To make our life divine requires an inner change of location, not an outer one.

What you have in life is God's gift to you. What you do with what you have is your gift to Him – Swami Chinmayananda

The mind catcher

"What should I do?" cried one man to Guruji. "My mind keeps running to bad thoughts."

"Take no notice," said Guruji.

"What!"

"Let me tell you a story from my younger days, when I was a brahmacārī," said Guruji. "I would often go visiting. One family was very excited to see me. 'Brahmacārī ji! Oh! You've come, how wonderful! Welcome, welcome to my home. Please sit down.' And the family man asked his wife to bring some tea, snacks and sweets."

"The wife gave a look of caution. But her husband ignored her, and continued to pour much affection on me. 'I am so happy you have come,' he said."

"I was tickled pink. I had given the man so much joy, I thought to myself. A few days later, I went to visit the same family again."

"'Brahmacārī ji, nice to see you,' said the man. 'Here,

have some tea and snacks.'"

"I wondered why there was no sweet served this time, and maybe, the welcome was less enthusiastic in general."

"The next week I went again. This time I was given only a cup of tea."

"The time after that, even the tea disappeared. But I still went again. 'Hari Om!' I said, knocking on the door once more. The family man took no notice. He continued to read his newspaper."

"'Hari Om!' I said again, and again. No one took notice. Finally, I came away. When I was outside the gate of the house, there was a jubilant scream: 'GONE! GONE!'"

"Likewise, you are entertaining your thoughts," continued Guruji, "by maintaining them, by liking or disliking them. Take no notice! Understood?"

"And," said Guruji, "don't ask me if this story is true!"

Thoughts come to an end when you don't pay any attention to them. Thoughts should not be suppressed, nor should they be fuelled; they should merely be witnessed in a detached way. As the predominant thoughts exhaust themselves, one must identify with the pure Self, and stand firm as a detached witness of the thoughts rising and passing away. By this practice, agitations in the mind will start to subside.

Don't get lost in your thoughts. Let your thoughts get lost in you – Swami Tejomayananda

What's in a name?

What does 'Prakāśa' mean? It means 'light'. When we say 'Prakāśa', everyone thinks of light. But someone named 'Prakāśa' will not think of 'light'. Instead, his attention will go to himself. In the same way, each appellation of the Supreme should be immediately perceived to be oneself.

We normally identify our names with our physical body, or the concept of who we think we are – that is, the Jīva (individuality). A man may be named Rāma, but his actions might be like Rāvaṇa. The name could be Balabīra, meaning strong and courageous, but the man might be such a weakling, that he could be blown away. But that is not the case with the Supreme Self. It is exactly as it is called – Sat-Cit -Ānanda. Sat is the name of the Self, because the Self is the Truth behind all illusions. The Self is Cit, because it is of the name of Consciousness. The Self is Ānanda, since it is the veritable source of all happiness. Thus, when we say Sat, Cit or Ānanda – or any other name given to the Self – we should not think of them (existence, consciousness, bliss and so on) as just intellectual concepts outside of ourselves, but each name should indeed be taken to be one's own self. Remember, we will not be true to our name Sat-Cit -Ānanda as long as we identify with the body or the individuality!

Always a
question mark

Yet again, the disciple had a question, so he went to Guruji.

"Guruji, I have a doubt I would like to ask," he said.

"Why ask me!?"

"But it is about your lecture, Guruji," said the disciple.

"There are so many excellent ācāryas[1] here," said Guruji. "They also attended my lecture. You can ask them."

The disciple continued to insist.

"I tried asking others," he said. "But I have not got an answer."

"I am not trying to avoid answering your question," said Guruji. "But you have been in study classes for a long time. How long will you keep asking questions? You must think for yourself. Think! *I want to break this dependence.* Real education must make you fearless, independent and self-reliant."

[1]teachers

Śravaṇa (listening) is to determine and grasp the essential teaching of the Scriptures. This is the first step in the ascent to the Truth. In the second step, there is mananam (reflection). The essential points gained from śravaṇa are made doubt-free by reflection. To merely question others will not erase doubts or give clarity to our understanding. For any real understanding, we need to think independently, introspect. Only then can it become a conviction.

In the third step, nididhyāsana (contemplation), the seeker strengthens the presence of the teaching in his heart by devoted single-pointed repetition of the assimilated understanding, in order to remove, shake off or shatter contrary habits formed in the past.

Rule of patience

One time in Uttarkashi, when Guruji went for bhikṣā,[1] he was introduced to a particular family member.

"Guruji, my brother is an acclaimed jyotiṣi,"[2] said the lady of the house, pointing to her brother. "People come from all over to ask him questions."

"Oh! Then I will also ask you a question," said Guruji to the astrologer.

"Very well," said the astrologer. "But you must not tell me the question. You keep it in your mind. I cannot give you the answer, but I will ask Bhagavān Gaṇeśa.[3] He will answer you.

Guruji silently asked the question in his mind and the astrologer started to make some calculations. He had an unusual method of doing calculations. He would get the answer after reading many caupāīs.[4]

[1]offering of food | [2]astrologer | [3]son of Śiva and Pārvatī. He is the remover of obstacles, the God of intellect and wisdom | [4]verses from Scripture

A little while later, the astrologer told Guruji: "The answer Bhagavān Gaṇeśa has given is...

...Wait!"

After reflecting for a bit, Guruji replied: "I think the answer is correct!"

The first response might be to trivialize the answer given by the astrologer. But on further reflection, it becomes clear, that as long as a person has a question, *any* question, the answer *is* 'Wait!' If we have understood and accepted the law of cause and effect in its entirety, then each moment is perfect. Nothing happens before time, or after it's time. Everything and each moment in creation is exactly how it should be, where it should be.

Give *you,*
get *Me* free

Guruji was sitting among many devotees at the Chinmaya Heritage Centre, Chennai, when someone offered him a basket of fruit with an envelope. When he lifted the envelope to put it on a side table, a one rupee coin fell on the floor.

One girl sitting nearby picked it up, and was about to give it back to Guruji.

"You keep it!" said Guruji light-heartedly.

"Wow! Guruji, they say a million dollars is like a penny to God!" she exclaimed. "How much is *your* rupee worth?"

"I am free, not cheap!" answered Guruji. "It is priceless!"

God or the Absolute Reality is free, because it is our essential nature. It is ever present, and without *It* we cannot exist. Just as air is free and we cannot put any value to it; in the same way, we cannot fix a price on existence itself. *It* is priceless!

Inside out
wisdom

The spiritual seeker and the man of the world stand poles apart in comparison. One soars high by the inward pull of his higher nature, and the other spins himself into the abyss of saṁsāra, by the outward pull of his lower nature.

The spiritual seeker, who has had enough of the outside world, will not waste his time on the trifles of the day, but will seek the eternal within. This is the serious business of life. All other things are secondary. Making a living is necessary, but it is not the purpose of life. This moment, this concept, this Truth, is the most tremendous Truth of life.

Life is made up of this moment and this moment only – not of dead yesterdays nor of unborn tomorrows. It is this moment. Moment to moment is illumination attained. Moment to moment enlightenment is brought about. Moment to moment is ultimate liberation experienced. Moment to moment is the supreme goal achieved.

The empirical
in the Absolute

Guruji was teaching the Māṇḍūkya Kārikā in the morning class.

"Not real, not real… this world is not real."

Every morning he continued: "Not real, not real… " again and again.

One student got fed up. The world looked very real to him. The next morning, after the class, he confronted Guruji.

"How can you say *not real!* If the world is *not real,* then why are you teaching?"

"Well," said Guruji, "my teaching is also *not real*".

From the standpoint of the absolute, the entire world is an illusion. Even Īśvara (total intellect) exists only from the standpoint of the jīva (individual ego). All plurality is only an appearance, like a rope mistaken for a snake. It is not that the jīva is identical to Brahman. It is Brahman alone that appears as the jīva. Jīvattva[1] is only an appearance. Brahmattva[2] alone abides. Brahman lone is, one without a second. It is the Reality. It is the Truth. And the ultimate teaching of the Upaniṣads and Vedānta is: *Brahma satyaṁ jaganmithyā jīvo brahmaiva nāparaḥ.* Brahman alone is the Reality, the world is an illusion; the jīva is nothing other than Brahman.

---

[1]principle of jīva, individual ego | [2]principle of Brahman, the Infinite Self

Alone to the alone
all alone is the way

A devotee had spent a week with Guruji, attending all the functions of the jñāna yajña.[1] On the last day, her eyes were full of tears at the thought of saying goodbye to him.

She went along with the many mission members to bid him farewell at the airport. As Guruji was about to walk towards the gate, he took her hand and walked with her until they reached the gate, after which only passengers are allowed entry.

Then he turned around, and lovingly said to her: "In life, people will be with you up to a point. After that, you have to walk alone."

Each individual is squarely responsible for his own happiness. The process of self-improvement must be executed by the individual through his own self-effort. No Guru can take the responsibility; no Scripture can

[1] series of spiritual discourses

promise this progress. Scriptures and Guru serve merely to guide; their job ends there. The mother can cook for the child, but the child has to eat by himself. The mother cannot eat for the child. So too, sādhanā (spiritual practice) must be done by the seeker alone.

From a higher standpoint of contemplation, in order to reach the One, all duality must be left behind. All props in any form – be it the world of things, relations, emotions or thoughts – have to be left behind to reach the Indivisible Truth. In the final ascent to divinity, there can be no division in the mind, not even of object and subject. It is in this division-less thought (akhaṇḍākāra-vṛtti) that the knowledge of the Self takes place.

The wandering minstrel

After the mind has been quietened to an extent – by methods such as observing the breath – the meditator initiates japa, or chanting of the Lord's name. As long as the chanting continues, the mind and intellect exist, since the mind is the thought flow, and the intellect, the discriminating faculty, which distinguishes one thought from another. In a concentrated spell of chanting, the meditator draws consciousness away from mind activity and creates a gap of no-mind in which he is highly alert and aware, but not thinking. This moment of dynamic silence, where neither the mind nor the intellect exists, is the state where the meditator, the meditated, and the meditation merge into one blissful experience. To abide in this state is to drift into the state of the pure Self.

This no-mind (no thought) state is the experience of pure awareness, with no distracting objects – only the infinite Self. This is the goal to be reached, the Truth to be realized, the experience divine to be lived as the meditator's own essential Self. It is not a thing to be objectively recognized or even intellectually comprehended. This state of no thought is to be spiritually apprehended, and it happens only on the mind's disappearance. The immediate experience: *that Self am I* – is the realization.

Dance of the
delectable

A rational minded medical doctor was quizzing Guruji at his brother's house in Rochester, where Guruji had come for breakfast.

"Have you had any sākṣātkāra?"[1] he wanted to know.

"No," was the reply.

"Have you witnessed any camatkāra?"[2]

"No," replied Guruji.

"Then how do you recognize God?" he asked.

"Jagat kāraṇam Īśvaram. God is the only cause and every effect in the world.

He is the causeless cause of all things. I do not have any sākṣātkāra or camatkāra. Hamārā sirpha namaskāra hai."[3]

---

[1]direct experience | [2]miracle | [3]Mine is only a prostration (to the Almighty)

Experiences that we may get in meditation are projections of the mind. Experiences come and go, since what comes must necessarily go. The seeker must remain as the silent witness of these passing experiences: *I am the pure Self, the silent witness of these passing experiences.*

The seeker may experience some strange things – some of a million varieties of possibilities are: enthralling visions, fascinating sounds, pleasant smells, melting touches and delicious tastes. The seeker must reject them all and rise above them.

The goal is to make our false identity with the ego totally disappear, and to identify with the eternal Self. This mystical experience of the transcendental is a thing apart. When the knowledge of the Truth takes place, the seeker comes to see God everywhere and in everything. Thus, the statement: *my namaskāra to the all pervading Reality.* Thereafter, temporary glimpses, visions or experiences have no meaning, for they have been left behind at the level of the mind. The realization of the Truth that God is everywhere can only take place once the seeker has transcended the body, mind and intellect.

When the identification with the body disappears and the Supreme Self is known, wherever the mind goes, there one experiences meditation. **Dṛg Dṛśya Viveka, Verse 30**

In the twinkling
of an eye

Some small children gave Guruji a card. It was like a playing card, except that it had a picture on it.

"Guruji, can you tell us what picture this is?" said one child very innocently.

"Let me see," replied Guruji.

He looked at the card. "It looks like a meadow and flowers, or something..." he said vaguely.

All the children started laughing.

"Papa, Mummy! Come see! Guruji doesn't know! Guruji doesn't know!" they shouted gleefully.

"Guruji, it's a cow!" shrieked one child. "Don't you see it?"

Guruji looked again. He did not see any cow. He looked and looked, and looked some more. No cow! Dinner was announced, but all through the meal his mind kept going to the playing card. He ate quickly and then came back to look again.

All of a sudden, he saw it! "There it is!" he pointed.

It was so clear and easy. Now, even if he wanted, he could not see anything but the cow!

"This is how it is with Self-Realization," he mused. We have been told by the śāstras[1] and the Guru that our true Self is pure, Infinite Consciousness. But when we sit down to meditate, we cannot see it. But if we keep looking, then suddenly, one day it is revealed to us. And after that, even if we want, we cannot see anything other than Consciousness."

In *Kenopaniṣad,* this is the description of Brahman (description by means of an illustration): *He shone forth like the splendour of lightning. He disappeared within the twinkling of an eye.* **Mantra 4.4**

Here is an example of the vividness of the experience, when knowledge of the Truth takes place. In the vision of Truth, nothing else remains as known or unknown but *THAT,* One without a second. Truth alone is, and the God experience is: *That I am.*

The illustration of the twinkling of an eye shows how natural and effortless is the final flight to the beyond in meditation. All efforts in meditation are only at the beginning

[1]scriptures

stages. When knowledge dawns, it is in fact a simple natural progression that tips (the seeker) into a state of 'everything'. In the moments of the final 'experience', the seeker comes to understand the omnipotent presence of the Self. And even after the 'experience' goes away, the knowledge of the Truth remains. Once this knowledge has taken place, it cannot be taken away. The moment the rope is recognized as a rope, the snake is not there.

The paradoxical nature
of Consciousness

"Guruji, I see *nothing!*" exclaimed someone. "If I see the world as not real, then I see nothing. So how can I also see myself as *everything* too? *Which* is right?"

"It is the same thing," replied Guruji. "You either become all, or you become zero. Since most people want to become something, they see themselves as everything. Alternately, some will see nothing."

"And, if you become something; that is really nothing. If you become nothing; then that is everything. This is a peculiar paradox of spiritual life."

At Self-Realisation, the Self is known as Brahman, that is, everything. We see our Self in all, in everything, and all and everything in our Self. At the same time, the jīva bhāva (sense of individuality) is no more, a zero. Thus, as Brahman we become everything; and as the jīva (individual ego) we become nothing. In becoming nothing (no jīva), we have also become everything (all pervading Reality, Brahman).

If we practice the bhāva[1] of being all, we become everything; and if we practice the bhāva of *Lord, I am nothing;* we become nothing. Both are complete. In fact, being *nothing* and being *everything* is the same.

---

[1]feeling

Supercalifragilistic
expialidocious

The Self cannot be understood through the instrument of the intellect, since the Self is behind the very functioning of the intellect. It is what illumines the body-mind-intellect equipment. The seer cannot be perceived through the very instruments of perception. The subject cannot become the object, just as the man behind the telescope cannot be the object of the telescope. To say that *I have understood the Self* through the intellect, is to make the Self into a conditioned object, whereas the Self is the 'Knowing Principle' because of which everything is known.

At the same time, the Man of Wisdom can neither say that he knows or does not know the Self. For example, an object other than oneself can be known by us 'well' or 'not so well'. But, the knowledge of oneself is through and through. That is, it is beyond or more than the knowledge of our son, wife, etc. We cannot say that we do not know our own self. Self-knowledge is a million times more subjective and too deep to express in words. Words can only convey knowledge through a series of references to known experiences. Thus, the Self cannot be understood by any equipment. It can only be known or recognized by being the Self itself.

The mighty
illusion

One evening in Sandeepany Sadhanalaya, Powai, Guruji was answering some questions about his recent poor state of health.

"Guruji, why did you get a stroke?"

"Don't ask why," he said. "It is inexplicable."

"But your B.P. was not abnormal and your cholesterol and triglycerides were in control. Then why?"

"Who knows? It is inexplicable."

"Is it because of the fruit and salad diet, Guruji?" asked another person.

"Without this diet, it would have happened much before," replied Guruji. "I am recovering quickly because of the diet."

"Guruji, maybe it is because of the 'honeymoon period in medicine'. B.P. patients feel extremely good after they first take the medicines. When their health improves, they stop. Then suddenly it comes crashing down… the honeymoon period!"

"But there are people who have not stopped for even a day, yet they get strokes right in front of the doctor!" exclaimed Guruji. "I tell you, it is inexplicable!"

The discussion slowly drifted to the recent hurricane in the United States.

"Guruji, water is creating havoc everywhere this year," said someone. "There were rains in Gujarat and Maharashtra, Katrina in the US, and now there are floods in Andhra, and another hurricane expected near Houston. Why?"

"Inexplicable!" said Guruji. "Everything is inexplicable! The Lord's māyā![1] He alone knows. We may give any number of reasons, but they are only apparent and superficial."

"How am I sitting and talking to you? Inexplicable! Who is talking through this body? Inexplicable! If you give answers, there will be assumptions with them."

"Science gives us theories, but there are always assumptions with them. If you question the assumptions, the theory collapses. Nothing is explicable. It is all inexplicable!"

"One imagines that one knows the answers to questions. Yet, the doubts that were there before the advent of knowledge seem to linger and persist. Things don't look that

[1]cosmic delusory power of the Lord

crystal clear when investigated closely. What is this mind? How does it function? I may intellectually know the answers, yet there is a mystery. In Vedānta when we ask: Why was the world created? Or why are we in bondage? We say: It is a logical illogicality! We never ask why? It is inexplicable!"

Māyā is the cosmic delusory power of the Lord. It is the very cause and sum and substance of creation.

Māyā is inexplicable. It cannot be described as existent or non-existent, one with the Lord or different from Him, made of parts or without parts, and so on. Indeed, anything and everything about māyā is inexplicable.

The world of names and forms, as well as the body, senses, mind and intellect are all products of māyā. As the cause, so the effect! It is therefore only natural that the effect – the entire world and everything that is or is not happening – remains inexplicable.

Abiding in this wisdom, the Man of Wisdom is quite content to see things as they are, without the hydra of 'why' raising its hood and polluting the free flow of serenity. He sees things as they are, and accepts the world as it is. Such relaxed living is the privilege of the Man of Wisdom alone. All others are mercilessly tossed about by the happenings of the world.

The way out of this māyā-maze is to rise above the intellect and stay as the Self, the very substratum of māyā. And lo! Then there is no māyā to be explained.

This divine illusion of Mine, made up of the guṇas (caused by the qualities) is difficult to cross over; those who take refuge in Me, they alone cross over this illusion. **Bhagavad Gītā, Ch. 7 Verse 14**

Further, explanations can only be given by the intellect. The intellect too is born from māyā. To try and understand māyā or the world is to try to catch a thief with another thief – an unholy nexus alone is the result! All intellectual conclusions are therefore confusion worst confounded.

What is Truth?

This is the question asked by Naciketas to Lord Death in **Kaṭhopaniṣad :** *When a man dies, this doubt arises; some say he is, and some say he is not. Teach me the Truth.* **Mantra 1.1.20**

There are some schools of thinkers who have established that death is the end of all and there is nothing but a zero beyond it. There are others who accept, argue and establish that there is existence even beyond the grave. Which is correct?

Death here implies not only the death of the body, but essentially the death of the ego (sense of limited 'I'). However, all concepts of existence or non-existence, life or death, are only valid within the body-mind-intellect framework. Whereas, the Self is never born, therefore *It* never dies. *It* did not spring from anything, nor did anything spring from *It*. The body-mind-intellect from birth to death with all its finite modifications and qualities does not exist in the eternal nature of the Self. Existence has meaning only with reference to its opposite, non-existence. Just as the word 'light' has no meaning in the sun; similarly, 'life', 'existence' hold no meaning in the Self, which is Existence-Consciousness itself.

The all pervading Self is ever there during birth, growth, decay and death. It is the eternal principle behind all change, the constant witness of all change; and it is the real *YOU*. When the Upaniṣads declare – *That thou art* – the term *thou* does not refer to the physical entity 'you' of name and form (identified by the body-mind-intellect). *Thou* refers to *YOU* as the hidden, unknown seer of all things seen, the knower of all things known. Thus, *It* is *YOU* – the infinite Self.

The vanishing
tiger

"When, *when* will my suffering end?" someone asked Guruji.

"It is your dream," replied Guruji. "And *YOU* are the tiger."

It meaning 'life' is a dream projected by our own mind. The *tiger* meaning the 'sorrows in life', which threaten our happiness in the dream, is also created by the mind because of our attachment to the illusory dream world. Since life and sorrow is made up within our own mind, it can be controlled by the mind. Thus, we ourselves are the remote controller of our life. When we 'wake' up, the dream ends, and the tiger is gone.

All suffering in life is because of the mental projection of the ego (sense of limited 'I'). The ego identifies itself as a separate finite body; and because of our limitations as a finite body, we become selfish and thus suffer in the form of fear, anger, etc. As long as we have this false identification that we are the limited ego, we will continue to suffer. But when the identification is shifted to our true nature, which is the One Absolute Reality, one without a second, then the ego is removed. And, once the veil of ignorance is lifted, there can be no suffering.

Enjoy in Joy

Guruji was eating dāla-cāvala[1] with much relish during his mid-day meal. One lady was ill at ease, as he licked his plate clean with deft fingers.

"Did you eat?" he jovially asked her later.

"Yes, Guruji," she replied. "The food was very nice."

"Did you lick your plate clean?"

"Um... No! I didn't."

"Then what kind of eating is that?"[2]

The Man of Wisdom moves among objects of the world freely, without any fear of attachment, with perfect self-control. Only such a fearless man, who is not limited by his individuality (ego) can live each moment to its fullest in the expanse of his true nature, enjoying the illusory world for the game it is.

[1]lentils and rice | [2]original conversation in Hindi: To phira kyā khāyā?

Letting out
the fizz

"I wish you were not suffering!" said an anxious devotee, when Guruji had been unwell with a prolonged illness.

"No! Nothing doing!" remarked Guruji. "My bad karmas[1] are being exhausted. Why should I block that?"

In spiritual life, suffering is a healer. It frees you from the effects of your past negative actions. The logic being that the present situation is the culmination of our own past actions, which we are in fact exhausting with the passing of each moment. If we try to escape from the present, it will resurface again in the future. Since there cannot be any escape from the eternal law of cause and effect, which binds every individual in the universe, the smart man will not run away from present situations. He will live them out with acceptance, to the best of his ability, exhausting his prārabdha.[2]

[1]actions | [2]effects of past actions that have caused the present

From the standpoint of the Man of Wisdom, his body is the continuation of the body he had in the past, and one that has been taken up as ordered or determined by his previous vāsanās (inclinations or tendencies dictated by past desires). Even though he has transcended the body-mind-intellect equipment, he is content to remain in the experience of the Infinite Consciousness and live out the prārabdha of his body.

Prārabdha is very powerful for the realized man and becomes nought only through the exhaustion of its fruits; while the sañcita[3] and āgāmi[4] karmas are destroyed in the fire of Knowledge.
Vivekacūḍāmaṇi, Verse 454

---

[3]collective effect of all actions | [4]effects of past actions that are to accrue in the future

The zero
sum solution

Guruji was totally absorbed in answering his mail. A few people came and sat near him whilst he was still working at his desk. After some time, he sat back, relaxed and appeared satisfied.

"The jñānī,[1] while doing everything, does nothing," he exclaimed. "And by doing nothing, he does everything."

"Doing everything, but doing nothing is sannyāsa. Doing nothing, but doing everything is yoga. Both point to the same state, but with a slight difference."

True sannyāsa or renunciation is giving up the sense of doer-ship and enjoyer-ship. Thus, when an individual, even while actively engaged in action, gives up the sense of *I am doing such and such action to enjoy such and such result* - that is sannyāsa.

[1]*Man of Wisdom*

Yoga is the dissolution of the mind in the Self. Such an individual looks to be doing nothing because of his inaction, but the truth is far from it. Because he is established in the dynamic stillness of the Self, he remains the very womb of the entire cosmos. Such a focussed resting in the Self is the greatest of all action, and truly the most difficult of all actions. Hence, in doing nothing, he is doing everything.

Yoga is the mastery of the activities of the mind-field. Then the seer rests in its true nature. **Patanjali Yoga Sutra 1.1**

Whether it is sannyāsa or yoga, they are both the same. Both rest in the Self. The difference is in the externalities, and only superficial.

O Pandava, please know yoga to be that which they call renunciation (sannyāsa); no one verily becomes a yogī who has not renounced thoughts. **Bhagavad Gītā, Ch. 6 Verse 2**

The time hand of God

However much we are told that everything in the world is changing – including wealth, name, fame, health, etc. – but until and unless we experience it for ourselves, we are not convinced. It is only by the hand of God, through the various knocks we get in life, which ultimately make us truly understand the fleeting nature of all things.

Dead bees
on a cake

A little boy in Nairobi asked Guruji: "If I saw the world with your eyes, what would I see?"

"A world full of contradictions," said Guruji.

"There are babies waiting to be born; but also being aborted. Some people can't wait to marry; others can't wait for a divorce. On the one hand, doctors are prolonging life; yet elsewhere youth are committing suicide. There are youngsters who wish to join the Vedānta course, but their parents do not want it!"

What looks normal to the ignorant man is abnormal for the Man of Wisdom. What looks just right for the ignorant man feels totally wrong and misplaced for the wise man.

That which is night to all beings, in that the self-controlled man keeps awake; where all beings are awake, that is the night for the sage who sees. **Bhagavad Gītā, Ch. 2 Verse 69**

The world is full of contradictions, but we hardly notice them. This is because we ourselves are full of contradictions, and thus these contradictions do not seem to prick us. We have become comfortable in our stupor of ignorance, very much like the pigs that seem to be at ease lolling in the dirt!

The day these contradictions (both within ourselves and in the world around) become evident to us; that day we will have taken the first step in our spiritual journey.

Twice
upon a time

"Sometimes," said one devotee to Guruji, "when I look at you, I forget Gurudev completely!"

"That should never happen," replied Guruji. "You should only see Gurudev in me."

The highest form of Karma Yoga (path of action) is to only see God (or the Guru) functioning through you, and through others.

God dwells in the heart of all beings. Arjuna, thy God dwells in thy heart. And His power of wonder moves all things – puppets in a play of shadows, whirling them onwards in the stream of time.
Bhagavad Gītā, Ch. 18 Verse 61

For a sincere spiritual seeker, the focus of attention should be on the Gurutattva.[1] The seeker should not make the Guru

[1]Teacher principle

into an individual, but concentrate on the vision and mission of the Master.

The Guru is not a person; he is an institution –
Swami Chinmayananda

The motor, the driver
and the fuel

Guruji was pacing the length of the living room, humming an unfinished tune for *Tvaṁ hi no netā Tvaṁ hi no dātā,*[1] the lyrics of which he had recently composed. He mulled over several variations and, dissatisfied, delayed lunch for a second time.

"Oh! Yaha bhūpa rāga meṁ hai,"[2] he exclaimed and quickly turned towards the harmonium. He sat down and tried many key strokes; but no, they were not quite right.

"Come, come... we are already late for bhikṣā,"[3] he said. "This tune will need some more time."

After a great deal of effort and tussle over many more days, the lyrics were set to a beautiful melody.

"What made you finally get the inspiration, Guruji?" asked an onlooker.

"Source of inspiration is only one. My Bhagavān."[4]

[1]Prārthanā Gītam - a musical composition by Swami Tejomayananda |
[2]This is in rāga Bhūpa | [3]offering of food | [4]My Lord

A revelation can only take place by the grace of God. But what we *can* do is create the necessary conditions for inspiration to happen; by right effort, concentration, hard work and attuning ourselves to the Lord.

Who's giving
to whom?

One person came to Guruji for an interpretation on a point of technicality.

"Guruji, you are not my Guru.[1] My Guru is another person. How can I give gurudakṣiṇā[2] to you?"

"What you give is not your gurudakṣiṇā to me. It is my gurudakṣiṇā to Gurudev."[3]

When offering any work to the Lord, the thought should be: *I am an instrument in the Lord's (or the Guru's) hands. I work on His behalf. I surrender unto Him.* Thus, Guruji's response suggesting: *You have not offered it to me. You have offered it to Gurudev.*

Also, any offering must be to the Gurutattva[4] to essence of the Guru. Whether he is in the form of his Guru or any other form, the Guru is always One. God alone appears in the form of any Guru.

[1]teacher | [2]offering to the Teacher | [3]Swami Chinmayananda | [4]Teacher principle

I'm fine,
thank you

You sadhus have such an easy life - don't have to work, no bills to pay, no responsibilities.

Is the path of the sādhu easy or difficult? The answer is: it depends. It depends on the angle you look at it from.

The Upaniṣads compare the path to walking on a razors's edge. It is difficult, because the goal here is the most challenging, for the conquest of the mind is indeed very difficult. But it is easy too, for all that is required for achieving this is clarity in thinking. Nothing external is required for achieving this – no wealth, family, power, and so on.

The sādhu is not bound by the fickle world and its changing concepts of 'good' and 'not good'. A lack of external dependence is a characteristic feature of the sādhu. But then, if that is the natural inclination or tendency of a person, then he cannot be otherwise. If one is a sādhu within, then one would be comfortable being a sādhu in the 'exterior' too. It all depends on how one is inside. Hence, for a sādhu, being a sādhu is neither easy nor difficult – for a sādhu is just being himself.

That said, others can have their own opinions according to their limited thinking. And this too is not an issue with the sādhu. And, why should the sādhu trouble himself to contradict what is seemingly a futile exercise?

The whole world
in my palms

Think naught a trifle, though it small appear, small sands the mountain, moments make the year.[1]

"Vivekji, how long have you been in the Mission?"

"Ten years," replied Brahmacārī Vivek Chaitanya.[2]

"In these ten years, what have you gained?"

"What I have gained is that I have stopped asking the question *What will I gain?* My life is beautiful. I just do what comes to me and enjoy it. I have gained fulfilment. *What is to be done, I have done. What is to be gained, I have gained.*"[3]

The Man of Wisdom is no longer dependent on the world (things, relationships, emotions, etc.) for his fulfilment and happiness. He has recognized that he has nothing to achieve, nowhere to go, for he is *all* and *everywhere*. He revels in total fulfilment for there is no want to become anything.

[1]quote by Edward Young | [2]Guruji's name as a brahmacārī | [3]*Bhagavad Gītā , Ch. 15 Verse 20*

Secret
of the deep

In the year 2005, Guruji was diagnosed with a serious illness. Many devotees were concerned for him.

"Guruji, you don't seem at all worried," said one devotee. "Who can you go to with your problems?"

"Where does water from the lake go?" countered Guruji.

"Umm... to the river," replied the devotee.

"Where does water from the river go?" he asked again.

"The ocean."

"Now, where does water from the ocean go?"

"Um... ?"

"Nowhere! Ocean water does not go anywhere. It takes refuge in its own depth."[1]

---

[1]original conversation in Hindi: Samudra kā pānī kahīṁ nahīṁ jātā. Vaha apanī geharāī meṁ samā jātā hai.

The Man of Wisdom, being established in the Self, gets his strength from the fullness and serenity (and stillness) of the Self itself (ocean), and tiny ripples on the surface cannot trouble him.

Moreover, there can be a clash between two waves (two jīvas), but where is the question of the ocean (totality, Īśvara) clashing with the wave when he sees the wave to be himself? The Man of Wisdom draws strength from knowing that he is not the wave, but the serene ocean.

The sannyāsi in whom the sense objects channelled by others are received like flowing rivers into the ocean producing no change because of his absorption in Existence Absolute, is truly liberated.
Vivekacūḍāmaṇī, Verse 442

Veparvāha!

During one of his trips to the Philippines, Guruji was presented with a 'wrinkle free' orange cloth by someone. Intrigued,
he immediately had himself measured and sent it to the tailor
to be stitched. Three days later, the clothes were ready to be
worn.

Quickly, he put them on. Then, in front of everybody
present, he suddenly jumped on the bed and rolled himself...
once... twice... three times.

Everyone was befuddled.

"What are you doing, Guruji?" asked one person.

"I was just checking if it is wrinkle free!"

In the Japji Sahib,[1] the Man of Wisdom is described as
Veparvāha, meaning carefree and detached. Whatever his
action, he is detached – ever free and ever joyous – for he has

[1]beginning verses by Guru Nānak Dev in the Guru Granth Sāhib

no attachment to the fruit of action.

There is perfect spontaneity both in children and in the perfect seer. They have no capacity to drag the past into the present, nor do they colour the present happenings with suspense of the future. The Man of Perfection lives from moment to moment, and lives fully and entirely in the chaste present. He carries no regrets from the past, nor does he have any anxiety for the future. Right here and now, like children ever do, the Man of Wisdom lives and revels.

Nonchalance

"Guruji, what would be the reaction of the knower of Brahman to experiences of the world?"

Guruji was standing on the stage, just about to leave, when he replied: "You see the world as though you were awake in a dream".

Then, looking left and then right, he said with amusement: "Your response to all your experiences would be: *Is that so! Is that so!*"

The Man of Wisdom is unaffected by the happenings of an illusory world. Neither is there any crisis, nor is there any joy; neither success nor failure. All situations are known to be so much of delusion, so much of illusion which never existed.

Who is balanced in blame and in praise; who is silent, who is happy with whatever he has; whose home is not in this world, and who has devotion – that man is dear to Me. **Bhagavad Gītā, Ch. 12 Verse 19**

Total contentment
of a Jīvanamukta

As I was sitting in my chair,
I knew the bottom wasn't there;
nor legs nor back, but I just sat,
ignoring little things like that.

The ability to live patiently through minor or major physical or mental inconveniences is one of the qualities of a Man of Wisdom. He is utterly detached from the equipments of the body, mind and intellect, and has cast away all desires. He enjoys the bliss of the Self and sees the world and its play of events as an illusion; thus he remains completely unaffected by them.

I am
where I am

A teenage devotee who had travelled across the continent to be with Guruji in Chinmaya Vibhooti ran to find him, when she found out that he was leaving.

"Guruji, I have come here only for you, and you are leaving me!"

Guruji smiled.

"Actually," he said, "I never go anywhere".

The teenager was not consoled.

"Everyone loves you, but I love you the most," continued Guruji.

He rhymed an old Hindi movie song, altering the second line:

>"Āja jāne kī zida nā karo
>(Today, don't insist on going),
>
>Yū hī kamare mem baiṭhe raho
>(Like that, in the room keep sitting)."

"Maiṁ apane kamare meṁ baiṭhā hūṁ
(I am sitting in my room),

 Aba mujhe kahīṁ nahīṁ jānā hai
(Now I do not have to go anywhere),

Aba mujhe kucha nahīṁ karanā hai
(Now I do not have to do anything),

Maiṁ apane kamare meṁ baiṭhā hūṁ
(I am sitting in my room)."

"Guruji, you have such a busy itinerary," remarked one bystander. "How can you not be going anywhere?"

"Kyukī (Because)," he said playfully, "Maiṁ apane kamare meṁ baiṭhā hūṁ (I am sitting in my room)".

Standing still He overtakes those who run. **Īśāvāsya Upaniṣad, Mantra 4**

That the Self is 'motionless' is an indication of the all-pervasiveness of the Supreme Reality. Motion is a change in time and space. A thing can go to another place only if it is not already there. Similarly, the Self does not and need not move anywhere, because there is no place where it does not already exist. Thus, the statement: *I never go anywhere.*

The Self is not only All-pervading, but it is the very substance and dynamism in all movements, and the very force behind every activity in life. All transactions in life can only take place, if presided over by the Self. The Self is Life, and without *It*, everything is dead and non-existent. Since the very nature of the Self is existence-consciousness, it does not have to *do* anything to *be*, for it always is. Thus, the statements: *I am sitting in my room. I do not have to go anywhere. I do not have to do anything.*

Love can only be total when it is for the Self. The Upaniṣads declare that it is not for the love of a person that a person is dear, but for the love of the Self that the person is dear. Love is conditional when there is a sense of separateness. Since the Man of Wisdom sees the Self in all, his love is unconditional and total. Also, since the love by the Man of Wisdom is an expression of the complete Self-experience and does not rise from the limited individual ego; his love is total as well. Thus, the statement: *I love you the most.*

Whichever way
the wind blows

From the standpoint of the Man of Wisdom, there are no 'goals' to be aspired or reached. To the one living in the Self, all worldly goals have no meaning or purpose. He has no more duties, for there can be no duty without identification with the individuality or jīva. Such a man lives in the world, until the prārabdha karma (result of past actions) of his body is finished. And as such, he flows with whatever comes to him in life, never asserting *his* will (the will of the individual ego, jīva) on anything. Whenever he is goaded to act in the world, it is due to his prārabdha, and he does so willingly, as an agent of the Lord, the Self.

From the standpoint of the seeker, the significance of flowing with the wind is accepting the will of God or the laws set in nature. Just as fire cannot turn cold and go against its essential nature which is heat; similarly, we cannot go against our dharma, which is existence, consciousness and bliss, and hope not to reap the consequences. As long as we continue to assert our ego into the play of events *(I am the doer, I can do anything I want)* in our present, or try to escape from the law of cause and effect set in nature, we will continue to suffer. It is not because of some freak accident that we find ourselves in any particular situation or condition in life. It is our own vāsanās (desires), and karmas (actions) in the past that have precipitated the present circumstance. As long as we do not accept this, we are moving away from our essential nature (dharma), and we will continue to be lost in the world.

Transliteration and Pronunciation Guide

In the book, *Devanāgarī characters are transliterated according to the scheme adopted by the International Congress of Orientalists at Athens in 1912. In it one fixed pronunciation value is given to each letter; f, q, w, x and z are not called to use. An audio recording of this guide is available at http://chinmayamission.com/scriptures.php. According to this scheme:*

	sounds like			sounds like
a	o in son		t	(close to) think
ā	a in master		th	th in thumb
i	i in if		d	th in then
ī	ee in feel		dh	the in breathe
u	u in full		n	n in numb
ū	oo in boot		p	p in purse
ṛ	ri in rim		ph	ph in loop hole
ṝ	(long ṛ)		b	b in but
e	ay in play		bh	bh in abhor
ai	y in my		m	m in mother
o	o in over		y	y in young
au	ow in now		r	r in run
k	k in kind		l	l in luck
kh	kh in blockhead		v	v in avert
g	(hard) in gate		ś	sh in shut
gh	gh in log-hut		ṣ	s in sugar
ṅ	ng in sing		s	s in sir
c	ch in chuckle		h	h in house
ch	chh in catch him		ṁ	(nasalisation of previous vowel)
j	j in jug		ḥ	(half h) (aspiration of preceeding vowel)
jh	dge in hedgehog			
ñ	n in banyan		ḻ	(close to 'world')
ṭ	t in tank		kṣ	ctio in action
ṭh	th in ant-hill		tr	th in three
ḍ	d in dog		jñ	gn in gnosis
ḍh	dh in godhood		'	a silent 'a'
ṇ	n in under			

Glossary

Ācārya	teacher
Ādi Śaṅkara Nilayam	maternal home & birthplace of Śrī Ādi Śaṅkarācārya
Āgāmi karma	effects of actions in present that will accrue in the future
Akhaṇḍākāra-vṛtti	division-less thought: *I am Brahman*
Ammā	lady (in general); often an elderly lady
Ānanda	Bliss
Ātman	Self
Balabīra	strong, courageous
Betā	son
Bhagavān	Lord, God
Bhajana	hymn
Bhāva	feeling
Bhūpa	name of a rāga in Indian classical music
Bhikṣā	offering of food
Brahman	Infinite Self, Ultimate Reality
Brahmacārī	one pursuing the knowledge of Brahman, one who lives a student life
Bhrama cārī	one on the path of illusion
Brahmattva	principle of Brahman
Caitanya	Consciousness
Camatkāra	miracle
Caupāī	verse from scripture
Cit	Consciousness

Dāla-cāvala	lentils & rice
Dāso'ham	I am His servant
Dharma	nature of a thing, duty, righteousness
Gaṇeśa	son of Śiva and Pārvatī, the remover of obstacles, God of intellect and wisdom
Gopīs	female devotees of Lord Kṛṣṇa from the cowherd clan
Guru	Teacher
Gurudakṣiṇā	offering to the Teacher
Gurutattva	Teacher principle
Jñāna yajña	series of spiritual discourses
Jñānī	Man of Wisdom
Iṣṭa devatā	chosen form of God for worship
Īśvara	Lord
Japa	repetitive chanting of Lord's name
Japji Sahib	beginning verses by Guru Nānak Deva in the Guru Grantha Sāhib-sacred scripture of Sikhs
Jīva	individual ego
Jīvattva	principle of individual ego
Jīva bhāva	sense of individuality
Jīvanamukta	one who is liberated while living
Jyotiṣi	astrologer
Karma	fruit of action, action
Kuṭiyā	small house
Mahāvākyas	statements in Upaniṣads revealing identity of Self with supreme Brahman
Mananam	reflection
Marāṭhī	dialect spoken in the Indian state of Maharashtra
Māyā	cosmic delusory power of the Lord; illusion; ignorance of the Self
Namaskāra	greetings

Nārāyaṇa	Lord Vishnu, the sustainer
Nārāyaṇa bhāva	feeling, thought or remembrance of God (Nārāyaṇa)
Nididhyāsana	contemplation
Om	sound symbol representing the Lord
Prakāśa	light
Prārabdha karma	effects of past actions that have caused the present
Prārthanā Gītam	a composition by Swami Tejomayananda
Prasāda	blessing
Rāga	musical composition
Rajas	characteristic of māyā which expresses as restlessness and desire and causes the misapprehension of Reality
Rāmāyaṇa	story of Lord Rāma
Ṛṣi	sage
Sañcita karma	collective effects of all actions
Sādhanā	spiritual practice
Sādhu	mendicant
Sākṣātkāra	direct experience
Samādhi	absorption of mind in the *I am Brahman* thought
Saṁsāra	movement, denotes cycle of birth and death
Saṅgata	assembly of body-mind-intellect and so on
Sannyāsa	path of renunciation
Sannyāsi	renunciate
Sat	Existence
Satsaṅga	company of the wise and pure
Sattva	characteristic of māyā which expresses as knowledge and serenity and leads to discrimination of Reality

Sevā	selfless service
Śāstra	scriptures
Siddhis	mystical powers
So'ham	I am *That*
Śravaṇa	listening to scriptures
Svadharma	one's natural inclination, duty
Tamas	characteristic of māyā which expresses as ignorance and stupor and causes the non-apprehension of Reality
Titikṣā	cheerful endurance or forbearance of all experiences
Upanayanam	thread ceremony
Upaniṣad	portion of scriptures that contain Knowledge of the Self
Vairāgya	detachment, dispassion
Vāsanās	habitual tendencies; impressions gained from past inclinations or tendencies dictated by past actions
Vedānta	literally 'end of Vedās', term denotes philosophy of the Upaniṣads
Veparvāha	detached, carefree
Vidyāmāyā	the Lord's power which expresses as love for the Divine
Viveka	discrimination
Yoga	the general practice of spirituality, often this word is used to denote the practice of the system of spiritual practices advocated by Patanjali called Raja-Yoga
Yogī	the one who is practicing Yoga

Did you know?

Spread over 70 acres of land in Kolwan, near Pune, Chinmaya
Vibhooti is a towering tribute to the founder of Chinmaya Mission,
Swami Chinmayananda, and the vision centre of Chinmaya Mission.
V I P – vision, inspiration, practice!
☏ 91 (20) 2296 0013 ⏐ chinmaya.vibhooti@chinmayamission.com

CHINMAYA INTERNATIONAL FOUNDATION

CIF is a centre of academia and research for Sanskrit and Indology in
the birthplace of Śrī Ādi Śaṅkarācārya, Veliyanad, Kerala.
☏ 91 (484) 274 7307 ⏐ office@chinfo.org ⏐ www.chinfo.org

CHINMAYA INTERNATIONAL RESIDENTIAL SCHOOL

CIRS is home to 550 students from 23 states of India and 18 countries.
This residential school endeavors to raise children of quality and
purpose - to make them perfect citizens of the world.
☏ 91 (422) 261 5725 ⏐ info@cirschool.org ⏐ www.cirschool.org

CHINMAYA ORGANIZATION FOR RURAL DEVELOPMENT

CORD empowers rural India through vocational training,
education, income generation schemes and primary healthcare.
☏ 91 (11) 2461 6291 ⏐ cordheadoffice@gmail.com ⏐ www.cord.org.in

CHINMAYA NAADA BINDU

A residential school for classical Music and Dance for the preservation and
propagation of Indian Art in the tradition of the guru śiṣya paramaparā.
☏ 91 (20) 2296 0013 ⏐ chinmayanaadabindu@chinmayamission.com

JÑĀNA YAJÑAS

Find out details for these series of talks on various spiritual texts and
subjects held around the year from your local mission centre.

STUDY GROUPS

Weekly study groups for members of society who wish to benefit from the perennial wisdom of India's scriptures. Sessions help in the practice of mananam (reflection) and in gaining a clearer insight and understanding of scriptural fundamentals. You can join study classes at your local center.

BALA VIHAR

Send your children to the world's most renowned and systematic Vedāntic learning forum for children based on specially designed syllabi.
☏ 91 (22) 2857 2367

CHINMAYA YUVA KENDRA

A call to the younger generation - CHYK empowers youth with vision, values, and dynamism for success in all fields - so that they realize their latent and infinite inner potential.
☏ 91 (44) 2232 8149

SANDEEPANY SADHANALAYAS

Institutes where students learn Advaita Vedānta based on various scriptural texts, in a sacred and ancient tradition imparted in a gurukula setting. This two-year residential Vedānta course is conducted in English at Mumbai; in Hindi at Sidhbari, Himachal Pradesh and in various regional languages in other states of India.
☏ 91 (22) 2857 5805 | tct@chinmayamission.com

PUROHIT COURSE

An integrated course which trains young boys as priests for conducting rituals, temple-worship and other ceremonies. Students are also taught Sanskrit, Astrology and English.
☏ 91 (422) 261 5497 | purohitcourse@gmail.com

CCMT PUBLICATIONS

A state of the art publication division based in Mumbai with offices world-wide that caters to all age groups; with over a thousand titles for books, DVDs, CDs and audio cassettes.
☏ 91 (22) 2857 2367 | ccmtpublications@chinmayamission.com

CHINMAYA VISION PROGRAMME

CVP is a comprehensive education programme that integrates the best of Indian culture and Vedāntic philosophy with academic learning. CVP focuses on four main topics: Integrated development, Indian culture, patriotism and universal outlook.
☏ 91 (422) 261 5663 | ccmtec@gmail.com